CW00384682

PRACTISE MENTAL MATHS

for ages

Dear Parent,

Welcome to Practise Mental Maths 7-8.

Confidence with numbers is one of the most important skills children learn at school and this workbook is designed to boost your child's confidence by providing lots and lots of structured practice. The tests become progressively more difficult as you work through the book so your child can gradually improve their speed and accuracy. The contents of this book is closely matched to the Numeracy Framework and so supports what your child is learning at school.

The best way to use this book is in regular, short bursts when your child is in a positive mood and not too tired. We have deliberately kept the tests short with just ten questions in each test, split into three sections: **Warm up**, **Quick fire** and **Problem solver**. A small working out space is provided for the **Problem solver** question but remember to have some extra scrap paper available if your child needs more space. Answers are included at the back of the book for you to check your child's work. Always give lots of praise and encouragement so that these mental maths tests become a rewarding experience for you both!

Test 1

1. Double 13. _____

2. How many 5p coins are there in 20p? _____

3. $9 + 9 + 9 = ?$ _____

Quick fire

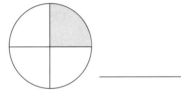

4. What fraction is the shaded part?

_____

5. Which number is half way between 40 and 50? _____

6. $2 + 4 = ?$ _____

7. $4 + 5 = ?$ _____

8. $6 + 2 = ?$ _____

9. $5 + 4 = ?$ _____

Problem solver

10. Bill had 50 marbles. Jen had 74 marbles.
    How many more marbles did Jen have?

_____

Test 2

Warm up

1. Draw a triangle in a square.

2. Circle the number which is a multiple of 2.

   9   11   13   16

3. What time would it be 10 minutes after 6 o'clock?

Quick fire

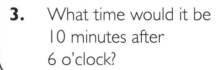

4. Find the difference between 25 and 35.

_____

5. Order these, starting with the smallest.   7, 2, 4, 6, 3

_____

6. $17 - 10 = ?$ _____

7. $10 - 7 = ?$ _____

8. $13 - 6 = ?$ _____

9. $12 - 4 = ?$ _____

Problem solver

10. Dan collected 32 conkers.
    Kira collected 23 conkers.
    How many did they have altogether?

_____

Test 3

Warm up

1. Circle the odd number.

    4   5   2   8   10

2. Divide each of these numbers by 2.

    4 ____   12 ____   10 ____

3. How many minutes are there in half an hour?

_____

Quick fire

4. Circle the numbers which you can divide exactly by 2.

    9   14   18   3   10   17

5. Circle the smaller number.

    38   62

6. $8 \times 2 = ?$ _____

7. $4 \times 2 = ?$ _____

8. $9 \times 2 = ?$ _____

9. $7 \times 2 = ?$ _____

Problem solver

10. Tariq picked 35 apples and 23 pears. How many fruits did he pick altogether?

_____

Test 4

Warm up

1. Which number is 5 more than 13?

_____

2. What time would it be 30 minutes after 8pm?

3. What is half of 80p?

_____

Quick fire

4. Continue the sequence.

    12   14 ____ ____ ____

5. Estimate the numbers on this line.

0   50

6. $16 \div 2 = ?$ _____

7. $20 \div 2 = ?$ _____

8. $14 \div 2 = ?$ _____

9. $18 \div 2 = ?$ _____

Problem solver

10. Jamie has a pack of 58 tomato seeds. He plants 24 seeds. How many are left?

_____

Test 5

1. What number is half of 12?

   _____

2. What do I add to 4 to make 24?

   _____

3. How many points are there on 3 triangles?

   _____

Quick fire

4. Continue the sequence of money.

   8p   10p   _____   _____   _____

5. Complete this calculation.

   $10 \div \boxed{} = 2$

6. $4 \times 2 = ?$ _____

7. $6 \times 2 = ?$ _____

8. $8 \times 2 = ?$ _____

9. $5 \times 2 = ?$ _____

Problem solver

10. Darla had 14 CDs. Bryony gave her 5 more. Then Darla gave Bryony 7 CDs. How many did she have left?

    _____

Test 6

1. Write this number in figures: Sixty two.

   _____

2. Write a number between 30 and 40 that is nearer 30.

   _____

3. What is half of 70cm?

   _____

Quick fire

4. Complete this calculation.

   $10 + \boxed{} = 17$

5. Estimate the numbers on this line.

   0 $\boxed{}$ $\boxed{}$ 100

6. $18 \div \boxed{} = 9$

7. $8 \div \boxed{} = 4$

8. $20 \div \boxed{} = 10$

9. $12 \div \boxed{} = 4$

Problem solver

10. A lion eats 30 kilograms of food each week. How much food would 5 lions need for a week?

    _____

Test 7

Warm up

1. Divide each of these numbers by 2.

   8   14   16

   _____   _____   _____

2. Choose the correct operation for this calculation.

   6 ☐ 2 = 8

3. What time would it be 10 minutes after 5pm?

Quick fire

4. What needs to be added to change 10 to 29?

   _____

5. Estimate the numbers on this line.

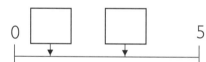

6. 6 + 3 = ? _____

7. 1 + 7 = ? _____

8. 2 + 8 = ? _____

9. 0 + 6 = ? _____

Problem solver

10. The sweet shop has 2 jars of liquorice sticks. Each jar holds 16 sticks. How many do they have altogether?

   _____

Test 8

Warm up

1. Circle the even number.

   38   27   9   13   43

2. Write an addition problem where the answer is 34.

   _____ + _____ = 34

3. 16 − 9 = ? _____

Quick fire

4. What needs to be subtracted from 60 to make 10?

   _____

5. What is the total?

   10 + 20 + 10 + 30 = ?

   _____

6. 12 − 4 = _____

7. 14 − 9 = _____

8. 16 − 8 = _____

9. 13 − 6 = _____

Problem solver

10. Pardeep is making apple pies. He needs 5 apples for each pie. How many pies can he make with 30 apples?

   _____

Test 9

Warm up

1. Circle the number nearest to 40.

    36   47   39   44

2. Write a subtraction problem where the answer is 12.

    _____ – _____ = 12

3. How many wheels are there on 3 cars?

    _____

Quick fire

4. Round these to the nearest 10.

    62   48   37   41   56

    ____ ____ ____ ____ ____

5. Order these, starting with the smallest.

    13   21   17   3   15

    ____ ____ ____ ____ ____

6. $6 \times 2 = ?$ _____

7. $7 \times 2 = ?$ _____

8. $3 \times 2 = ?$ _____

9. $8 \times 2 = ?$ _____

Problem solver

10. Sonja made 27 cards for the school Spring Fair. Her dad spilled his tea on 13. How many were left to sell?

    _____

Test 10

Warm up

1. Round 69 to the nearest 10.

    _____

2. Multiply 2 by 7.

    _____

3. Add 2 to each of these numbers.

    62   49

    _____   _____

Quick fire

4. Round these fractions to the nearest whole number.

    $2\frac{1}{4}$ _____ $3\frac{3}{4}$ _____ $5\frac{2}{3}$ _____

5. Circle the smallest number.

    12   13   11

6. $10 \div 2 = ?$ _____

7. $14 \div 2 = ?$ _____

8. $4 \div 2 = ?$ _____

9. $18 \div 2 = ?$ _____

Problem solver

10. Mr Hammond is setting out the tables for Parents' Evening. There are 4 rows of 8 tables. How many tables did he put out altogether?

    _____

Test 11

Warm up

1. Which number is 15 more than 8?

   _____

2. Write a pair of numbers which total 38.

   _____ + _____ = 38

3. $6 + \boxed{} = 15$

Quick fire

4. Continue the sequence of adding 2 to each number.

   43 _____ _____ _____ _____ _____

5. Order these amounts from the smallest to the largest.

   £0.47   £0.36   £0.25   £0.52

   _____ _____ _____ _____

6. $13 - 8 = ?$ _____

7. $14 - 5 = ?$ _____

8. $15 - 9 = ?$ _____

9. $16 - 8 = ?$ _____

Problem solver

10. Coral had 32 felt pens. She gave half to Sandra. How many did she have left?

    _____

Test 12

Warm up

1. What number is half of 28?

   _____

2. Which is less? 41 units or 4 tens?

   _____

3. What is one quarter of 20p?

   _____

Quick fire

4. Continue the sequence of fractions.

   4     $4\frac{1}{2}$ _____ _____ _____ _____

5. Estimate the months on this line.

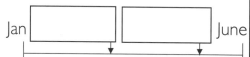

Jan | | | June

6. $8 \times 2 = ?$ _____

7. $10 \times 2 = ?$ _____

8. $4 \times 2 = ?$ _____

9. $5 \times 2 = ?$ _____

Problem solver

10. Tania feeds the horses 3 buckets of oats every day. How many does she need for a week?

    _____

Test 13

Warm up

1. Write the amount which is half of £1.40.

   _____

2. Write a multiplication problem where the answer is 12.

   _____ × _____ = 12

3. Subtract 4 from each of these numbers.

   | 11 | 12 | 13 |

   _____ _____ _____

Quick fire

4. How much money is this?

    × 40

   _____

5. What is the total?
   20 + 10 + 40 + 30 =

   _____

6. 40 ÷ 4 = ? _____

7. 60 ÷ 6 = ? _____

8. 20 ÷ 2 = ? _____

9. 30 ÷ 3 = ? _____

Problem solver

10. There are 40 stones on the beach. $\frac{1}{2}$ have holes in them. How many stones have holes?

    _____

Test 14

Warm up

1. Write the number which is half of 26.

   _____

2. Add 5 to each of these numbers.

   | 11 | 13 | 15 |

   _____ _____ _____

3. 3 × 4 = _____

Quick fire

4. Double these numbers.

   | 7 | 23 | 32 | 41 |

   _____ _____ _____ _____

5. What is the smallest number you can make with these digits?

   7, 3, 4 _____

6. 3 + 3 + 3 = ? _____

7. 5 + 5 + 5 = ? _____

8. 6 + 6 + 6 = ? _____

9. 2 + 2 + 2 = ? _____

Problem solver

10. Imagine a 0–20 number line. Which number is 3 to the left of 18?

    _____

Test 15

Warm up

1. Double 13.
   _____

2. What do I add to 15 to make 29?
   _____

3. 3 + 9 = ? _____

Quick fire

4. What fraction is the shaded part?

   _____

5. Continue this money sequence.

   15p   20p _____ _____ _____

6. 17 − 7 = ? _____

7. 11 − 1 = ? _____

8. 15 − 5 = ? _____

9. 18 − 8 = ? _____

Problem solver

10. Apple juice costs 40p. Orange juice costs 16p more. How much is orange juice?

    _____

Test 16

Warm up

1. Draw a circle inside a square.

2. Write a number between 40 and 60 that is nearer 60.
   _____

3. 26 ÷ 2 =
   _____

Quick fire

4. Count back in steps of 4 from 20.

   20 _____ _____ _____ _____

5. Estimate the numbers on this line.

   0 _____ 16

6. 16 × 2 = ? _____

7. 19 × 2 = ? _____

8. 14 × 2 = ? _____

9. 12 × 2 = ? _____

Problem solver

10. Gran went on a short cruise for 48 hours. How many days and nights was that?

    _____

Test 17

Warm up

1. Circle the odd number.

   43   28   36   70

2. Choose the correct operation for this calculation.

   27 ☐ 5 = 22

3. How many tails are there on 87 monkeys?

   _____

Quick fire

4. Circle the numbers which you can't divide by 4 exactly.

   8   13   12   16   24

5. Estimate the numbers on this line.

   0   ☐   ☐   20

6. 60 ÷ 10 = ? _____

7. 80 ÷ 10 = ? _____

8. 40 ÷ 10 = ? _____

9. 50 ÷ 10 = ? _____

Problem solver

10. Carrie is 12. Joanne is 3 years older than Carrie. Julie is as old as both of them together. How old is Julie?

    _____

Test 18

Warm up

1. What number is one fifth of 30?

   _____

2. 19 – 14 = ? _____

3. What is one quarter of 100 grams?

   _____

Quick fire
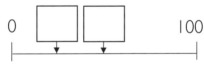

4. Which 3 coins could make 21p?

   _____ + _____ + _____ = 21p

5. Estimate the numbers on this line.

   0   ☐   ☐   100

6. 6 + 6 = ? _____

7. 6 + 5 = ? _____

8. 2 + 9 = ? _____

9. 7 + 4 = ? _____

Problem solver

10. Jane is twice as old as Jemima. Jemima is 8. How old is Jane?

    _____

Test 19

Warm up

1. Round 78 to the nearest 10.

   _____

2. Write a division problem where the answer is 4.

   _____ ÷ _____ = 4

3. Divide each of these numbers by 2.

   16   18   22

   _____   _____   _____

Quick fire

4. Which four coins could make 60p?

   _____ + _____ + _____ = 60p

5. Estimate the numbers on this line.

   0 [ ]   [ ] 20

6. 19 – 5 – 6 = ? _____

7. 17 – 6 – 4 = ? _____

8. 13 – 6 – 1 = ? _____

9. 16 – 8 – 2 = ? _____

Problem solver

10. Martin buys 4 stickers for his bike. They are 15p each. How much does he spend?

    _____

Test 20

Warm up

1. Round £1.37 to the nearest 10p.

   _____

2. Multiply each of these numbers by 2.

   6   12   13

   _____   _____   _____

3. What is half of 4 hours?

   _____

Quick fire

4. Find the missing numbers.

   _____   50   _____
   40   _____

5. Halve these numbers.

   16   26   46   66

   _____   _____   _____   _____

6. 9 x 5 = ? _____

7. 5 x 5 = ? _____

8. 8 x 5 = ? _____

9. 3 x 5 = ? _____

Problem solver

10. Jonathan needed some string for his kite. He tied 3 pieces together. The pieces were 30cm, 47cm and 32cm. How long was the string?

    _____

Test 21

Warm up

1. Write a subtraction problem where the answer is 9.

   _____ – _____ = 9

2. 30 + 30 + 30 = ? _____

3. What is one half of 16 grams?

   _____

Quick fire

4. Double these numbers.

   25   32   41   52

   _____ _____ _____ _____

5. Add these amounts:

   56p + 20p + 43p

   _____

6. 35 ÷ 5 = ? _____

7. 40 ÷ 5 = ? _____

8. 25 ÷ 5 = ? _____

9. 45 ÷ 5 = ? _____

Problem solver

10. Inderjit is half the age of Brian. Brian is 16. How old is Inderjit?

    _____

Test 22

Warm up

1. How many 10p coins are there in £2?

   _____

2. What is one half of 400?

   _____

3. What is the day after the day after Thursday?

   _____

Quick fire

4. What needs to be subtracted from 74 to make 50?

   _____

5. Which number is exactly halfway between 20 and 32?

   _____

6. $6 + 3 = \boxed{} + 4$

7. $5 + \boxed{} = 1 + 7$

8. $8 + 4 = 7 + \boxed{}$

9. $\boxed{} + 6 = 7 + 5$

Problem solver

10. Neil is twice as old as his brother Tim. Tim is 14. How old is Neil?

    _____

Test 23

Warm up

1. Write this number in words: 250

   _____

   _____

2. Divide each of these numbers by 10.

   40   70   90

   _____   _____   _____

3. How many minutes are there in half an hour?

   _____

Quick fire

4. Round these to the nearest £1.

   £3.17   £2.68   £4.40   £0.75

   _____   _____   _____   _____

5. Estimate the weights on this line.

   0   [ ]   [ ]   60g

6. 16 − 5 = ? _____

7. 14 − 6 = ? _____

8. 12 − 7 = ? _____

9. 11 − 5 = ? _____

Problem solver

10. Graham wants to buy a goldfish for his pond. Fish cost 87p each. Graham only has 50p. How much more does he need?

    _____

Test 24

Warm up

1. Circle the number which is half of 86.

   41   42   43   44

2. Multiply each of these numbers by 4.

   2   6   7

   _____   _____   _____

3. 20 + 30 + 40 = _____

Quick fire

4. Circle the numbers which are not multiples of 5.

   23   25   37   40   45   50   54

5. Circle the larger number.

   401   399

6. 4 × 3 = 2 × [ ]

7. 6 × [ ] = 3 × 8

8. 2 × 8 = 4 × [ ]

9. 6 × [ ] = 3 × 4

Problem solver

10. Calendar Challenge!

    What will the date be one week after July the 1st?

    _____

Test 25

Warm up

1. Circle the number which is not an exact multiple of 5.

   20   25   30   34   40

2. Write a division problem where the answer is 2.

   _____ ÷ _____ = 2

3. How many fingers and thumbs are there altogether on 4 hands?

   _____

Quick fire

4. Round the answer to the nearest 10

   137 + 40 = _____   _____

5. Complete this multiplication calculation.

   5 × ☐ = 35

6. 40 ÷ ☐ = 10

7. 40 ÷ ☐ = 4

8. 40 ÷ ☐ = 2

9. 40 ÷ ☐ = 20

Problem solver

10. Imagine a 0–20 number line. Which number is 11 squares to the right of 5?

    _____

Test 26

Warm up

1. Write this number in figures: three hundred and twenty four.

   _____

2. Write a pair of numbers which total 65.

   _____ + _____ = 65

3. How many minutes are there in two hours?

   _____

Quick fire

4. Find the difference between 24 and 13.

   _____

5. Complete this addition calculation.

   56 + ☐ = 63

   _____

6. 3 + 3 + 3 + 3 + 3 = ? _____

7. 3 + 4 + 3 = ? _____

8. 5 + 2 + 5 = ? _____

9. 7 + 6 = ? _____

Problem solver

10. Calendar Challenge!

    If today is Monday the 16th of December, what will be the date next Monday?

    _____

Test 27

Warm up

1. Circle the odd numbers.

   137   173   142   145

2. Which number is 125 more than 5?

   _____

3. 92 − 68 = ?

   _____

Quick fire

4. What needs to be added to 76 to make 101?

   _____

5. What is the total ?

   6ml + 21ml + 3ml + 5ml

   _____

6. 16 − 5 = 13 − ☐

7. 15 − 7 = 11 − ☐

8. 18 − 9 = 15 − ☐

9. 17 − 6 = 11 − ☐

Problem solver

10. Mystery numbers.
    We are both under 19. If you divide one of us by the other, the answer will be 9. Which 2 numbers are we?

    _____

Test 28

Warm up

1. Add 7 to each of these numbers.

   2   5   8

   _____ _____ _____

2. 35 ÷ 5 = ?

   _____

3. How many days are there in May?

   _____

Quick fire

4. Round the answer to the nearest 100

   126 + 60 = ?   _____ _____

5. How much is this?

       × 10 _____

6. ☐ × 5 = 20

7. ☐ × 5 = 45

8. ☐ × 5 = 30

9. ☐ × 5 = 25

Problem solver

10. Mike bought 2 bags of crisps. They were 35p each. How much did he spend?

    _____

Test 29

Warm up

1. Circle the number which is nearest to 140.

    139   142   145   150

2. Write a pair of numbers which total 84.

    _____ + _____ = 84

3. $5 +$ ☐ $= 140$

Quick fire

4. Round these to the nearest 10.

    12   78   126   97

    _____ _____ _____ _____

5. Order these from the smallest to the largest.

    115   105   125   120

    _____ _____ _____ _____

6. $20 ÷ 4 = ?$ _____

7. $20 ÷ 10 = ?$ _____

8. $20 ÷ 20 = ?$ _____

9. $20 ÷ 5 = ?$ _____

Problem solver

10. Bharti made 400ml of jelly. The jelly bowl holds 250ml. How much jelly was left after she filled the bowl?

    _____

Test 30

Warm up

1. Round 412 to the nearest 100.

    _____

2. Write a multiplication problem where the answer is 30.

    _____ × _____ = 30

3. $40 + 40 + 40 = ?$ _____

Quick fire

4. Round these fractions to the nearest whole number.

    $2\frac{1}{2}$ _____ $5\frac{3}{4}$ _____ $9\frac{3}{4}$ _____

5. Circle the smaller number.

    607   670

6. $3 + 5 = ?$ _____

7. $7 + 4 = ?$ _____

8. $9 + 1 = ?$ _____

9. $7 + 7 = ?$ _____

Problem solver

10. Peta cuts 35cm from a metre of ribbon. How much is left?

    _____

Test 31

Warm up

1. Which number is 41 less than 100?

_____

2. What is half of 70p?

_____

3. What time would it be 30 minutes after 5:10?

Quick fire

4. Continue the sequence by adding 4.

72 ____ ____ ____ ____ ____

5. Order these from the largest to the smallest.

£0.19   £0.29   £0.22   £0.27

____ ____ ____ ____

6. 24 − 9 = ? _____

7. 23 − 5 = ? _____

8. 32 − 8 = ? _____

9. 21 − 4 = ? _____

Problem solver

10. Megan collected 16 shells on the first day of her holiday, 27 shells on the second day and 43 on the third day. How many shells did she bring home?

_____

Test 32

Warm up

1. What do I add to 82 to make 100?

_____

2. Write a division problem where the answer is 6.

_____ ÷ _____ = 6

3. What is half of 90 centimetres?

_____

Quick fire

4. Continue the sequence of fractions.

$7\frac{1}{3}$ $7\frac{2}{3}$ ____ ____ ____ ____

5. Estimate the times on this line.

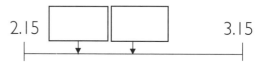

2.15 ___ ___ 3.15

6. 7 × 3 = ? _____

7. 5 × 3 = ? _____

8. 9 × 3 = ? _____

9. 4 × 3 = ? _____

Problem solver

10. Class 3 collected cans for charity. On Monday they brought 14, on Tuesday they brought 21, on Wednesday they brought 18. How many cans did they collect?

_____

Test 33

1. What is half of 90?

   _____

2. Choose the correct operation for this calculation.

   46 ☐ 16 = 30

3. 8 × 4 = ?

   _____

Quick fire

4. Halve these numbers.

   20   32   34   36

   ____ ____ ____ ____

5. Order these from the smallest to the largest.

   £2.12   £2.21   £2.14   £2.41

   ____ ____ ____ ____

6. 13 ÷ ☐ = 13

7. 26 ÷ ☐ = 13

8. 40 ÷ ☐ = 20

9. 120 ÷ ☐ = 10

Problem solver

10. The bus leaves school at 3.30. Mark arrives home at 4.00. How long is his journey?

    _____

Test 34

Warm up

1. What is half of 88?

   _____

2. 27 + 100 = ? _____

3. How many minutes are there in 3 hours?

   _____

Quick fire

4. Double these numbers.

   51   52   53   54

   ____ ____ ____ ____

5. What is the smallest number you can make with these digits?

   2   7   8   0   _____

6. 10 + 8 = ? _____

7. 9 + 7 = ? _____

8. 14 + 5 = ? _____

9. 12 + 7 = ? _____

Problem solver

10. Linda buys 3 plants for her Gran's window box. The plants are 25p each. How much does she spend?

    _____

Test 35

1. What do I add to 96 to make 100?

   _____

2. Write a number between 131 and 147 that is nearer 131.

   _____

3. Circle the number which is not an exact multiple of 10.

   204   240   260   280

Quick fire

4. What fraction is the shaded part?

   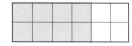   _____

5. Complete this sequence of money.

   £0.25   £0.50   _____   _____

6. $16 - 4 - 5 = ?$ _____

7. $18 - 6 - 5 = ?$ _____

8. $13 - 4 - 5 = ?$ _____

9. $17 - 4 - 7 = ?$ _____

Problem solver

10. Aaron cuts 45cm from a metre of foil. How much is left?

    _____

Test 36

Warm up

1. Draw a cube.

2. $40 \div 5 = ?$ _____

3. Add the number of days in July to the number of days in August.

   _____

Quick fire

4. Count on in steps of 4 from 91.

   91 _____ _____ _____ _____

5. Estimate the numbers on this line.

   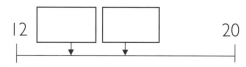

6. $90 \div 10 = ?$ _____

7. $40 \div 10 = ?$ _____

8. $70 \div 10 = ?$ _____

9. $30 \div 10 = ?$ _____

Problem solver

10. Imagine a 0 – 25 number line. Which number is 6 squares to the left of 21?

    _____

Test 37

Warm up

1. Which number is 97 less than 100?

   _____

2. $54 + \boxed{} = 84$

3. How many legs are there on 8 chairs?

   _____

Quick fire

4. Circle the numbers which can be divided exactly by 4.

   27   32   16   19   20   18

5. Estimate the numbers on this line.

   0 [ ][ ] 500

6. $11 + 11 + 11 = ?$ _____

7. $10 + 2 + 14 = ?$ _____

8. $10 + 14 + 16 = ?$ _____

9. $16 + 0 + 12 = ?$ _____

Problem solver

10. Doug had a charity garage sale. He sold 21 toy cars, 14 comics and 5 packs of game cards. How many items did he sell?

    _____

Test 38

Warm up

1. Which number is 40 more than 70?

   _____

2. $130 - 50 = ?$

   _____

3. What is one quarter of £2?

   _____

Quick fire

4. Complete this sequence.

   38   43 ____ ____ ____ ____

5. Estimate the measurements on this line.

   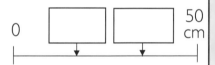

   0 [ ][ ] 50 cm

6. $17 - 4 - 4 = ?$ _____

7. $22 - 4 - 4 = ?$ _____

8. $15 - 4 - 4 = ?$ _____

9. $19 - 4 - 4 = ?$ _____

Problem solver

10. Caroline has 200cl of orange juice. How many 50cl lollies can she make?

    _____

Test 39

1. Circle the number which is nearest to 133.

   129   143   137   130

2. Write a subtraction problem where the answer is 27.

   _____ – _____ = 27

3. How many days are there in May?

   _____

Quick fire

4. Round the answer to the nearest 10

   86 + 47 = _____ _____

5. Estimate the numbers on this line.

   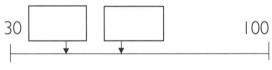

   30 [ ] [ ] 100

   Complete the sequences.

6. 40 50 60 ___

7. 15 25 ___ ___

8. 40 ___ 60 ___

9. 55 60 ___ ___

Problem solver

10. Ganesh visits his cousins 4 times a week. The return bus fare is 65p. How much does he spend on bus fares each week?

    _____

Test 40

Warm up

1. Round £8.99 to the nearest pound.

   _____

2. Add 100 to each of these numbers.

   7   4   21

   _____   _____   _____

3. Write the name of the third month of the year.

   _____

Quick fire

4. Find the missing numbers.

   127 ⟶ 138 ⟶ _____ ⟶ _____ ⟶ _____

5. What is the largest number you can make with these digits?

   3   5   2   6   _____

6. $30 \div \boxed{} = 15$

7. $20 \div 2 = \boxed{}$

8. $\boxed{} \div 10 = 4$

9. $80 \div 10 = \boxed{}$

Problem solver

10. Colleen had 16 sweets. She gave $\frac{1}{4}$ to her friend. How many did she have left?

    _____

20

Test 41

Warm up

1. What number is three quarters of 80?

_____

2. $32 + \boxed{} = 100$

3. Write the name of the month which comes after August.

_____

Quick fire

4. Round the answer to the nearest 10

$123 + 116 =$ _____   _____

5. How much is this?

 $\times 40$ _____

6. $6 + 12 = ?$ _____

7. $7 + 19 = ?$ _____

8. $4 + 13 = ?$ _____

9. $6 + 14 = ?$ _____

Problem solver

10. Kendo's glass holds 80ml of lemonade. It is half full. How much lemonade is in the glass?

_____

Test 42

Warm up

1. Which is more? 7 tens or 60 units?

_____

2. Multiply each of these numbers by 5.

7   9   5

_____   _____   _____

3. A ladder measured 3 of these. Underline the unit.

cm   km   m

Quick fire

4. Make 40 using 3 of these numbers.

15   16   7   17   3

_____ + _____ + _____ = 40

5. Which number is exactly halfway between 46 and 76?

_____

6. $28 - 3 = ?$ _____

7. $29 - 5 = ?$ _____

8. $21 - 4 = ?$ _____

9. $24 - 6 = ?$ _____

Problem solver

10. Gill's baby sister drinks 250cl of milk in each feed. She has 4 feeds each day. How much milk does she drink in a day?

_____

Test 43

1. Subtract 4 from each of these numbers.

    17   19   23

    _____   _____   _____

2. $7 +$ ☐ $= 109$

3. Write a pair of numbers which total 113.

    _____ + _____ $= 113$

Quick fire

4. Round these amounts to the nearest £1.

    £5.23   £3.87   £4.16   £7.98

    _____ _____ _____ _____

5. Estimate the weights on this line.

    0 [ ] [ ] 500g

6. $3 \times 2 \times 2 = ?$ _____

7. $5 \times 2 \times 2 = ?$ _____

8. $6 \times 2 \times 2 = ?$ _____

9. $4 \times 2 \times 2 = ?$ _____

Problem solver

10. Missing number.

    If you divide me by 10 the answer will be 7. Which number am I?

    _____

Test 44

1. What is half of 84?

    _____

2. Multiply each of these numbers by 4.

    7   3   10

    _____ _____ _____

3. What is half of £7?

    _____

Quick fire

4. Circle the numbers which are exact multiples of 4.

    25   28   31   36   40

5. Circle the larger number.

    899   988

6. $26 \div 2 = ?$ _____

7. $68 \div 2 = ?$ _____

8. $14 \div 2 = ?$ _____

9. $54 \div 2 = ?$ _____

Problem solver

10. Lyle buys 7 book club stamps at 4p each. How much did they cost?

    _____

22

Test 45

1. Write this number in words: 248

_____

_____

2. Circle the numbers which are not exact multiples of 4.

42   43   44   45   46   47   48

3. What time would it be 30 minutes before 7 o'clock?

Quick fire

4. Round these to the nearest 100.

487   519   649   727

_____   _____   _____   _____

5. Complete this division calculation.

$100 \div \boxed{} = 10$

6. $12 + 12 + 12 = ?$ _____

7. $14 + 12 + 10 = ?$ _____

8. $13 + 14 + 15 = ?$ _____

9. $15 + 10 + 5 = ?$ _____

Problem solver

10. Harry cut his apple into 4 equal pieces. What fraction was each piece?

_____

Test 46

Warm up

1. Circle the number which is nearest to 900.

880   940   916   890

2. Multiply 7 by 3.

_____

3. What is half of 120?

_____

Quick fire

4. Find the difference between 94 and 68.

_____

5. Complete this addition calculation and then write as a subtraction calculation.

$18 + 23 =$ $-$ $=$

_____   _____   _____   _____

6. $20 - 7 - 4 = ?$ _____

7. $20 - 9 - 3 = ?$ _____

8. $20 - 8 - 5 = ?$ _____

9. $20 - 12 - 7 = ?$ _____

Problem solver

10. Corrine borrowed 65p for the bus fare from her friend Rachel. She has 37p left from her pocket money. How much more does she need to pay Rachel back?

_____

Test 47

Warm up

1. Circle the even numbers.

    113   120   206   241

2. Write an addition problem where the answer is 98.

    _____ + _____ = 98

3. 20 × 4 = ? _____

Quick fire

4. What needs to be added to 96 to make 112?

    _____

5. Add these amounts.

    54p + £1.20 _____

6. 4 × 3 = ? _____

7. 7 × 2 = ? _____

8. 8 × 5 = ? _____

9. 9 × 10 = ? _____

Problem solver

10. Mystery numbers.

    One of us is double the other. If you multiply us together the answer is 18. What numbers are we?

    _____

Test 48

Warm up

1. Which number is 59 less than 100?

    _____

2. Write a number between 96 and 102 that is nearer 102.

    _____

3. 125 + 35 = ? _____

Quick fire

4. Make 40 using three of these numbers.

    5   17   13   18

    ____ + ____ + ____ = 40

5. Which four coins make 50p?

    ____ + ____ + ____ + ____ = 50p

6. 30 ÷ 2 = ? _____

7. 30 ÷ 5 = ? _____

8. 30 ÷ 10 = ? _____

9. 30 ÷ 1 = ? _____

Problem solver

10. Missing number.

    If you divide me by 4 the answer will be 7. Which number am I?

    _____

24

Test 49

Warm up

1. Round £6.19 to the nearest 10p.

   _____

2. Write a pair of numbers which total 75.

   _____ + _____ = 75

3. How many days are there in 4 weeks?

   _____

Quick fire

4. Round these to the nearest 100.

   537   499   602   999   838

   ____ ____ ____ ____ ____

5. Order these from the largest to the smallest.

   712   395   828   598

   _____ _____ _____ _____

6. 14 + 14 = ? _____

7. 12 + 19 = ? _____

8. 16 + 16 = ? _____

9. 19 + 11 = ? _____

Problem solver

10. Pam was playing a counter game on a square board with 100 squares. She put a counter on half the squares? How many counters did she use?

    _____

Test 50

Warm up

1. Write the number which is half of 98.

   _____

2. Write a subtraction problem where the answer is 36.

   _____ − _____ = 36

3. Circle the best unit to measure the weight of a mouse?

   kg   g   m   ml

Quick fire

4. Continue the sequence of fractions.

   $14\frac{1}{2}$ 15

5. Circle the smaller number in each pair.

   516   561   689   698

6. 35 − 5 = ? _____

7. 34 − 4 = ? _____

8. 33 − 5 = ? _____

9. 32 − 6 = ? _____

Problem solver

10. Albert has 85p. He wants to buy a comic which costs £1.45. How much more money does he need?

    _____

Test 51

1. What number is one quarter of 40?

   _____

2. 38 + $\boxed{}$ = 100

3. Look at this number.   1761
   Underline the hundred.

4. Continue the sequence by adding 8.

   8 ____ ____ ____ ____ ____

5. Order these from the smallest.

   £2.22   £2.12   £2.21   £2.32

   ____ ____ ____ ____

   Complete the sequences.

6. 90 80 ___ ___

7. 50 80 ___ ___

8. 70 ___ 80 ___

9. 60 ___ ___ 90

10. Elisa had some pet mice. 7 ran away.
    Now she has 18. How many did she
    have to start with?

    _____

Test 52

1. Which is more? 400 units or 41 tens?

   _____

2. Circle the numbers which are not
   exact multiples of 4.

   37   41   48   52   54

3. 127 + 50 = ? _____

4. Continue the sequence of fractions.

   $5\frac{2}{10}$ $5\frac{3}{10}$ ____ ____ ____ ____

5. Estimate the times on this line.

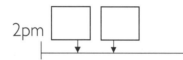

6. 90 ÷ 10 = ? _____

7. 120 ÷ 10 = ? _____

8. 160 ÷ 10 = ? _____

9. 80 ÷ 10 = ? _____

10. One of us is between 5 and 7. The
    other is between 8 and 12. If you
    multiply us the answer is 54.
    Which numbers are we?

    _____

Test 53

Warm up

1. Write the amount which is half of £1.20.

   _____

2. Write a division problem where the answer is 5.

   _____ ÷ _____ = 5

3. Divide each of these numbers by 4.

       4   40   100

   _____ _____ _____

Quick fire

4. What are the largest and smallest numbers you can make with these digits?   1   7   1   8

   Largest _____ Smallest _____

5. Order these from the smallest.

   £4.24   £4.54   £4.45   £4.42

   _____ _____ _____ _____

6. 17 + 17 = ? _____

7. 18 + 30 = ? _____

8. 19 + 15 = ? _____

9. 12 + 27 = ? _____

Problem solver

10. Sandy bought 2 comics at 60p each and 2 packets of football cards at 20p each. How much did she spend?

    _____

Test 54

Warm up

1. Write the number which is half of 112.

   _____

2. Choose the correct operation for this calculation.

   4 [   ] 2 = 2

3. Write a pair of numbers which total 99.

   _____ + _____ = 99

Quick fire

4. Double these numbers.

     36   42   58   69

   _____ _____ _____ _____

5. What is the smallest number you can make with these digits? 2 9 1 4

   _____

6. 22 − 4 = ? _____

7. 24 − 16 = ? _____

8. 34 − 15 = ? _____

9. 42 − 13 = ? _____

Problem solver

10. Beatrice's watch is 20 minutes fast. It says 5.20. What is the real time?

    _____

Test 55

Warm up

1. Double 300.

   _____

2. Write a number between 73 and 79 that is nearer 73.

   _____

3. Circle the numbers which are exact multiples of 10.

   40   72   90   120   85

Quick fire

4. What fraction is the shaded part?

   _____

5. Complete this sequence of money.

   £1.15   £1.21   _____   _____

6. $1 \times 5 = ?$ _____

7. $3 \times 5 = ?$ _____

8. $9 \times 5 = ?$ _____

9. $7 \times 5 = ?$ _____

Problem solver

10. Julie collects toy frogs. She gave 7 away to a charity sale, then she gave 3 to her best friend. She has 14 frogs now. How many did she have to start with?

    _____

Test 56

Warm up

1. Draw a circle in a square.

2. Write this number in figures: six hundred and fourteen.

   _____

3. Circle the number which is not an exact multiple of 3.

   30   33   36   38   42

Quick fire

4. Find the difference between 50 and 17.

   _____

5. Estimate the numbers on this line.

   42 [ ] [ ]   52

6. $60 \div 10 = ?$ _____

7. $60 \div 5 = ?$ _____

8. $60 \div 2 = ?$ _____

9. $60 \div 1 = ?$ _____

Problem solver

10. If an elephant eats 55 kilograms of hay every day, how much does it eat in 2 days?

    _____

Test 57

Warm up

1. Circle the odd numbers.

   467   468   472   473

2. What time would it be 15 minutes after 9.40?

3. What is the answer to this calculation chain?

   21 + 21 + 21 = ? _____

Quick fire

4. Circle the numbers which can be divided exactly by 10.

   223   240   190   367   450

5. Estimate the numbers on this line.

   500 [ ] [ ] 1000

6. 14 + 17 = ? _____

7. 19 + 21 = ? _____

8. 16 + 22 = ? _____

9. 15 + 24 = ? _____

Problem solver

10. Fallon bought a headband for £2.25 and 2 tennis balls for 60p each. How much did he spend?

   _____

Test 58

Warm up

1. Which number is 120 less than 300?

   _____

2. Write a multiplication problem where the answer is 40.

   _____ × _____ = 40

3. 320 – 140 = ?

   _____

Quick fire

4. Continue the sequence.

   20   24 ____ ____ ____ ____

5. Estimate the measures on this line.

   0 [ ] [ ] 200

6. 60 – 25 = ? _____

7. 45 – 10 = ? _____

8. 70 – 30 = ? _____

9. 45 – 5 = ? _____

Problem solver

10. Dawn was 10 minutes late for school. School starts at 8.55. What time did Dawn arrive?

   _____

Answers

Test 1
1. 26
2. 4
3. 27
4. $\frac{1}{4}$
5. 45
6. 6
7. 9
8. 8
9. 9
10. 24 marbles

Test 2
1. [triangle in square]
2. 16
3. [clock]
4. 10
5. 2, 3, 4, 6, 7
6. 7
7. 3
8. 7
9. 8
10. 55 conkers

Test 3
1. 5
2. 2, 6, 5
3. 30
4. 14, 18, 10
5. 38
6. 16
7. 8
8. 18
9. 14
10. 58

Test 4
1. 18
2. [clock]
3. 40p
4. 16, 18, 20
5. 20, 35
6. 8
7. 10
8. 7
9. 9
10. 34 seeds

Test 5
1. 6
2. 20
3. 9
4. 12p, 14p, 16p
5. 5
6. 8
7. 12
8. 16
9. 10
10. 12 CDs

Test 6
1. 62
2. 31-34
3. 35cm
4. 7
5. 20, 80
6. 2
7. 2
8. 2
9. 3
10. 150 kilograms

Test 7
1. 4, 7, 8
2. +
3. [clock]
4. 19
5. 1, 3
6. 9
7. 8
8. 10
9. 6
10. 32 sticks

Test 8
1. 38
2. Accept any two numbers that total 34.
3. 7
4. 50
5. 70
6. 8
7. 5
8. 8
9. 7
10. 6 pies

Test 9
1. 39
2. Accept any two numbers that when subtracted equal 12.
3. 12
4. 60, 50, 40, 40, 60
5. 3, 13, 15, 17, 21
6. 12
7. 14
8. 6
9. 16
10. 14 cards

Test 10
1. 70
2. 14
3. 64, 51
4. 2, 4, 6
5. 11
6. 5
7. 7
8. 2
9. 9
10. 32 tables

Test 11
1. 23
2. Accept any two numbers that total 38.
3. 9
4. 45, 47, 49, 51, 53
5. £0.25, £0.36, £0.47, £0.52
6. 5
7. 9
8. 6
9. 8
10. 16 felt pens

Test 12
1. 14
2. 4 tens
3. 5p
4. 5, 5$\frac{1}{2}$, 6, 6$\frac{1}{2}$
5. March, May
6. 16
7. 20
8. 8
9. 10
10. 21 buckets

Test 13
1. £0.70 or 70p
2. 3 × 4, 4 × 3, 1 × 12, 12 × 1, 2 × 6, 6 × 2
3. 7, 8, 9
4. 40p
5. 100
6. 10
7. 10
8. 10
9. 10
10. 20

Test 14
1. 13
2. 16, 18, 20
3. 12
4. 14, 46, 64, 82
5. 347
6. 9
7. 15
8. 18
9. 6
10. 15

Test 15
1. 26
2. 14
3. 12
4. $\frac{5}{8}$
5. 25p, 30p, 35p
6. 10
7. 10
8. 10
9. 10
10. 56p

Test 16
1. [circle in square]
2. 51-59
3. 13
4. 16, 12, 8, 4
5. 8, 13
6. 32
7. 38
8. 28
9. 24
10. 2

Test 17
1. 43
2. —
3. 87
4. 13
5. 10, 15
6. 6
7. 8
8. 4
9. 5
10. 27 years old

Test 18
1. 6
2. 5
3. 25 grams
4. 2 × 10p, 1 × 1p
5. 25, 50
6. 12
7. 11
8. 11
9. 11
10. 16 years old

Test 19
1. 80
2. Accept any two numbers which when divided equal 4.
3. 8, 9, 11
4. 2 × 20p, 2 × 5p, 2×10p
5. 5, 15
6. 8
7. 7
8. 6
9. 6
10. 60p

Test 20
1. £1.40 or 140p
2. 12, 24, 26
3. 2 hours
4. 30, 60, 70
5. 8, 13, 23, 33
6. 45
7. 25
8. 40
9. 15
10. 109 cm

Test 21
1. Accept any 2 two numbers which when subtracted equal 9.
2. 90
3. 8 grams
4. 50, 64, 82, 104
5. 119p or £1.19
6. 7
7. 8
8. 5
9. 9
10. 8 years old

Test 22
1. 20
2. 200
3. Saturday
4. 24
5. 26
6. 5
7. 3
8. 5
9. 6
10. 28 years old

Test 23
1. Two hundred and fifty
2. 4, 7, 9
3. 30
4. £3, £3, £4, £1
5. 15g, 30g
6. 11
7. 8
8. 5
9. 6
10. 37p

Test 24
1. 43
2. 8, 24, 28
3. 90
4. 23, 37, 54
5. 401
6. 6
7. 4
8. 4
9. 2
10. July the 8th

Test 25
1. 34
2. Accept any two numbers which when divided equal 2.
3. 20
4. 177, 180
5. 7
6. 4
7. 10
8. 20
9. 2
10. 16

Test 26
1. 324
2. Accept any two numbers which total 65
3. 120 minutes
4. 11
5. 7
6. 15
7. 10
8. 12
9. 13
10. 23rd December

Test 27
1. 137, 173, 145
2. 130
3. 24
4. 25
5. 35ml
6. 2
7. 3
8. 6
9. 0
10. 18, 2

Test 28
1. 9, 12, 15
2. 7
3. 31
4. 186, 190
5. 50p
6. 4
7. 9
8. 6
9. 5
10. 70p

Test 29
1. 139
2. Accept any two numbers which total 84

3. 135
4. 10, 80, 130, 100
5. 105, 115, 120, 125
6. 5
7. 2
8. 1
9. 4
10. 150ml

Test 30
1. 400
2. Accept any two numbers which when multiplied equal 30
3. 120
4. 3, 6, 10
5. 607
6. 8
7. 11
8. 10
9. 14
10. 65cm

Test 31
1. 59
2. 35p
3. 5:40
4. 76, 80, 84, 88, 92
5. £0.29, £0.27, £0.22, £0.19
6. 15
7. 18
8. 24
9. 17
10. 86 shells

Test 32
1. 18
2. Accept any two numbers which when divided equal 6
3. 45
4. 8, 8⅓, 8⅔, 9, 9⅓
5. 2.30, 2.45
6. 21
7. 15
8. 27
9. 12
10. 53

Test 33
1. 45
2. –
3. 32
4. 10, 16, 17, 18
5. £2.12, £2.14, £2.21, £2.41
6. 1
7. 2
8. 2
9. 12
10. 30 minutes

Test 34
1. 44
2. 127
3. 180 minutes
4. 102, 104, 106, 108
5. 2078
6. 18
7. 16
8. 19
9. 19
10. 75p

Test 35
1. 4
2. 131-139

3. 204
4. ⅔ or 8/12 or 4/6
5. £0.75, £1.00
6. 7
7. 7
8. 4
9. 6
10. 55cm

Test 36
1.
2. 8
3. 62
4. 95, 99, 103, 107
5. 14, 16
6. 9
7. 4
8. 7
9. 3
10. 15

Test 37
1. 3
2. 30
3. 32
4. 32, 16, 20
5. 250, 325
6. 33
7. 26
8. 40
9. 28
10. 40 items

Test 38
1. 110
2. 80
3. 50p
4. 48, 53, 58, 63
5. 17, 35
6. 9
7. 14
8. 7
9. 11
10. 4 lollies

Test 39
1. 129
2. Accept any two numbers that have a difference of 27
3. 31 days
4. 133, 130
5. 40, 60
6. 70
7. 35, 45
8. 50, 70
9. 65, 70
10. 260p or £2.60

Test 40
1. £9
2. 107, 104, 121
3. March
4. 149, 160, 171
5. 6532
6. 2
7. 10
8. 40
9. 8
10. 12 sweets

Test 41
1. 60
2. 68
3. September

4. 239, 240
5. 80p
6. 18
7. 26
8. 17
9. 20
10. 40ml

Test 42
1. 7 tens
2. 35, 45, 25
3. m
4. 7, 17, 16
5. 61
6. 25
7. 24
8. 17
9. 18
10. 1000cl or 1L

Test 43
1. 13, 15, 19
2. 102
3. Accept any two numbers which total 113
4. £5, £4, £4, £8
5. 100g, 300g
6. 12
7. 20
8. 24
9. 16
10. 70

Test 44
1. 42
2. 28, 12, 40
3. £3.50
4. 28, 36, 40
5. 988
6. 13
7. 34
8. 7
9. 27
10. 28p

Test 45
1. Two hundred and forty-eight
2. 42, 43, 45, 46, 47
3.
4. 500, 500, 600, 700
5. 10
6. 36
7. 36
8. 42
9. 30
10. ¼

Test 46
1. 890
2. 21
3. 60
4. 26
5. 41, 41 – 23 = 18
6. 9
7. 8
8. 7
9. 1
10. 28p

Test 47
1. 120, 206
2. Accept any two numbers that total 98
3. 80

4. 16
5. £1.74
6. 12
7. 14
8. 40
9. 90
10. 3, 6

Test 48
1. 41
2. 100-101
3. 160
4. 5, 17, 18
5. 2 × 20p, 2 × 5p
6. 15
7. 6
8. 3
9. 30
10. 28

Test 49
1. £6.20
2. Accept any two numbers that total 75
3. 28 days
4. 500, 500, 600, 1000, 800
5. 395, 598, 712, 828
6. 28
7. 31
8. 32
9. 30
10. 50

Test 50
1. 49
2. Accept any two numbers with a difference of 36
3. g
4. 15½, 16, 16½, 17
5. 516, 689
6. 30
7. 30
8. 28
9. 26
10. 60p

Test 51
1. 10
2. 62
3. 1761
4. 16, 24, 32, 40, 48
5. £2.12, £2.21, £2.22, £2.32
6. 70, 60
7. 110, 140
8. 75, 85
9. 70, 80
10. 25 mice

Test 52
1. 41 tens
2. 37, 41, 54
3. 177
4. 5 4/10, 5 5/10, 5 6/10, 5 7/10
5. 2.30, 3pm
6. 9
7. 12
8. 16
9. 8
10. 6, 9

Test 53
1. £0.60
2. Accept any two numbers that when

divided equal 5.
3. 1, 10, 25
4. 8711, 1178
5. £4.24, £4.42, £4.45, £4.54
6. 34
7. 48
8. 34
9. 39
10. £1.60

Test 54
1. 56
2. –
3. Accept any two numbers which total 99.
4. 72, 84, 116, 138
5. 1249
6. 18
7. 8
8. 19
9. 29
10. 5:00

Test 55
1. 600
2. 74-75
3. 40, 90, 120
4. 7/10
5. £1.27, £1.33
6. 5
7. 15
8. 45
9. 35
10. 24 frogs

Test 56
1.
2. 614
3. 38
4. 33
5. 44, 46
6. 6
7. 12
8. 30
9. 60
10. 110 kilograms

Test 57
1. 467, 473
2.
3. 63
4. 240, 190, 450
5. 625, 750
6. 31
7. 40
8. 38
9. 39
10. £3.45

Test 58
1. 180
2. Accept any two numbers which when multiplied total 40
3. 180
4. 28, 32, 36, 40
5. 50, 100
6. 35
7. 35
8. 40
9. 40
10. 9.05